MICHAEL SLAVIN

The Father of the Bride: A Survival Guide

How to Keep Your Sanity and Wallet Intact

To Greer, my amazing and wonderful daughter who made me a Father of the Bride. Thank you for being the great woman you are.

I used to think a wedding was a simple affair. Boy and girl meet, they fall in love, he buys a ring, she buys a dress, they say I do. I was wrong. That's getting married. A wedding is an entirely different proposition...

GEORGE BANKS, THE FATHER OF THE BRIDE, 1991

Contents

Prelude

FOTB Survival Tactic #1 – Don't abdicate your position. The "whatever you want, dear" response can cost you. Be interested, involved, and supportive.

Hello there...

If you are reading, and hopefully buying this book, you fall into a category with over 2.1 million other people per year in the US. This special class of people has a wedding to plan. If you aren't the prospective father of the bride, then you are most likely either the mother or the bride looking to help the father get through this event. I have been where you are now; I understand your feelings and fears.

Before going any further, I want to acknowledge that the terms "bride" and "groom" have evolved to encompass an expanded acceptance of sexual preferences and declarations in our society. Today, there are many different configurations for weddings based on regional, religious, and cultural preferences. Because it is not possible to consider all, this book is based primarily on what I've come to understand are traditional structures and divisions of responsibilities for wedding activities and financial support.

As I reflected on my experience as a father of the bride, I regarded the years raising my daughter before her engagement as just a warm-up to the main event – a pressure-filled cauldron otherwise known as a wedding. If you are a father like me, you are probably not equipped to face all that is entailed in planning a wedding, and fear the engagement period will be an unbridled, emotionally-driven money fest.

When my only daughter decided to get married, I was terrified at the prospect. I vaguely knew the range of dollars families spent on weddings, sizes of invitation lists, and had heard stories of families at each other's throats. The vision of handing over my checkbook to a wedding planner scared me more than a full IRS audit.

Other than providing funding for what I perceived would be a multi-month-long circus, there didn't seem to be a role or duty for me. And I was very careful not to intrude on the wedding team with unwelcome opinions or suggestions. So, I faded into the background and waited for my cue from the team.

For months, the wedding took over all the attention, emotions, and focus of the family's ecosystem. Every day seemed to be greeted with some new ultra-time-sensitive decision to be made, or even worse, a disaster du jour harder to solve than a Rubik's cube.

Often, I wished for someone to provide me with the guidance, assurance, and confidence needed to be the best possible father of the bride. Being a process-driven, problem-solving creature by nature, I sought to lean on my business experience. I craved a timeline, checklists, decision criteria, and status calls to make everyone feel at ease when so much was on the line. That is what I felt I needed; a coach to demystify the process, identify and help navigate the probable potholes, and role-play the tough conversations and negotiations that would inevitably occur. I could have benefited from someone who could communicate in my terms.

The Father of the Bride: A Survival Guide is a father-centric roadmap and coaching tool on how to survive and actively participate in the wedding process. Based on experience with a dash of humor added, the book will provide a future FOTB with insight into:

- Roles the father of the bride is expected to play
- Approaches on the all-important budgeting and money questions
- Identifying and controlling the key wedding cost drivers
- Strategies for defusing emotional emergencies
- Avoiding wedding-planning fatigue and keeping things in perspective
- Where the father of the bride might make a difference

If all goes well yours will be a great wedding and a day of incredible memories for family and friends. The icing on the cake is getting the special thank-you hug or kiss from the bride as she parts from you to her new life.

The journey I propose is divided into three acts: the planning cycle, event preparation, and the wedding.

Act One: The Planning Cycle begins at the moment of the engagement announcement. This act is highlighted by the magical appearance of people and tasks all seemingly needing immediate decisions, approval, and funding —at least in the form of down payments. All the major dimensions of the wedding are addressed some way early in this act. The FOTB needs to understand what these are, the timings, cost impacts, and emotional weight of:

- The planning team
- Venue
- Number of invitees
- Timing
- Budget

The most important thing for the FOTB in **Act One** is to understand and help to keep the scope and decisions as simple as possible, minimizing downstream risk.

Act Two: Event Preparation, is the building of the wedding. This is the longest part of the wedding process, characterized by possible disasters and in-flight changes. Given most engagements are longer than pregnancies, there are bound to be emotional breakdowns and break-ups during the long Act Two. For most, the concept of the wedding being real doesn't occur until the end of the act, when the major social events are concluded, the bride is perhaps in possession of her gown, and gifts are beginning to arrive.

In addition to big-ticket items such as choice of the venue and apparel, the largest and most critical task for FOTB and team is attendance management. Managing an accurate list of attendees is one of the largest emotional and financial pieces of the wedding.

Act Three: The Wedding, is the payoff for all the hard work in the preceding months. Just like a large project or military offensive, everything seems to happen at once. The FOTB and team need patience, a plan, and a good sense of humor to make the best of the day. This act is made up of the concrete items to be managed to completion, like flowers, food, liquor, and entertainment. There is a whole other set of tasks around managing the social event of the wedding and the reception. I will discuss and help the FOTB with two of his major contributions for the day: the FOTB speech and the father's dance with the bride.

The purpose of **The Father of the Bride: A Survival Guide** is quite simple—to offer suggestions for more easily managing the process of getting to that thank-you kiss sanely, with coaching and guidance. This book provides you with some tools and references to support your journey to a memorable day for you, the mother of the bride, the engaged couple, family, and friends.

FOTB Survival Tactic #1 – Don't abdicate your position. The "whatever you want, dear" response can cost you. Be interested, involved, and supportive.

Act One: The Planning Cycle

Setting the Stage

When does planning for a wedding begin? Well, most likely it started several years ago when your daughter first experienced sexual attraction and began to dream about what the future might hold.

The fun begins when the future son-in-law pops the question and puts a good bit of his earnings on your daughter's ring finger.

The first couple of weeks of an engagement really do set the direction, scope, tenor, and overall character of the wedding. The initial scope of the affair is determined by understanding the couple's desires and thoughts about timing, venue, and number of attendees. At this juncture, your job as father of the bride is to LISTEN with great interest as initial thoughts spew forth like a caffeinated geyser of wedding-speak. You must be diplomatic, ask clarifying questions, constantly nod your head to indicate, "I hear you", but avoid verbal commitments until all the puzzle pieces can be discussed. Keep all options open until the really serious process of planning begins... and I will get to that in a bit.

You may already know your future in-laws. Perhaps your kids went to school together and you've spent time with them. Most likely you are just going to meet them for the first time. Either way, the stakes in the game have moved up. No longer are the relationships just casual, with only passing social politeness needed to make it through a weekend, a dinner, or some event our children got us all into. No, my friend. This time the stakes are much bigger: you are setting the stage for a relationship that is supposed to last until at least the end of your life. The in-laws are the people you will be sharing your children— and possibly grandchildren—with. You will be jockeying for time on the kids' calendar for holidays and other visits. There will be countless social events, dinners, birthdays, etc. you may attend together. Hours and days will be spent in the same space with the in-laws.

You will engage in debates about who gets what grandparent name. The grandparent's name issue sounds distant, especially since your child isn't married yet, but time flies, and it is important to make an effort to get along well, as the in-laws will be in your life forever.

If it has been agreed that both families will take part in the wedding planning, one of the most important reasons for the initial meeting with the in-laws after the engagement is to hear their thoughts about the event. As the largest financial contribution is traditionally dependent on the bride's family, the question to the groom's family is about their thoughts on how many people should be invited. Attendance (butts in seats) is the number one cost driver for a wedding. Again, your job as the FOTB is to listen, share in the in-laws' hopeful joy about the event, and compliment them on having raised a quite wonderful person.

Ah yes, the future son-in-law… almost forgot about him. Hopefully, you've gotten to know this person for quite a while and have started to picture him as a potential member of the family. A son you never had, or maybe a complement to one you do have. The opposite is a bad and hard place to be in. Obvious and hardened disapproval of the prospective groom will not gain any points with your daughter and will create a more painful engagement period. Remember, you've got many months before the ceremony to find a way to accommodate and tolerate each other.

To the point of earning respect, on my wedding day, my soon-to-be father-in-law had a short and pointed message for me. Before the ceremony, he found me and whispered in my ear, "never hit her." He was old school and wanted me always to treat his daughter with love and respect. And if I didn't, I would pay dearly.

As you reflect on the expanse of the wedding journey ahead of you, it is very important to ask yourself and others a single question: who is the wedding for? Many will say the wedding is all about the bride and groom and it is their day. Others will tell you it's about family and friends coming together. And the truth is that both answers are correct. In the arc of a family's history, there are two key events that most often bring everyone together: weddings and funerals. One is the joyful launching of a new part of the greater family, while the other is a respectful remembrance of the part someone played in the family.

Not everyone will agree, but there is a larger picture you must see as you plan the wedding. Putting aside the pride or love you have for your child, there is a responsibility to friends and family to create a positive and lasting memory.

FOTB Survival Tactic #2 – Learn how to say "no" diplomatically. There are multiple, interdependent segments of the wedding to be weighed against each other. Logic and emotion must be balanced.

Scene One – Establish the Planning Team

Like any good project, your wedding needs a planning team. It is important to establish the team composition along with roles at the beginning. Traditionally, the core or central team is made up of the bride and the mother of the bride. They are the ones with the most vested in all the decisions and have the patience to go through the vast number of choices needing to be made over the coming months.

Your wedding may be one where the bride and groom lead the way. They may be leading in terms of financial contribution, or just really be wanting to take the reins. In this scenario, to determine the level of interaction taking place, much is going to depend on the type of relationship the bride has with her family. You will have a role, but most of the day-to-day concerns will be on the shoulders of the bride and groom. Nonetheless, keep reading, as it is very important for you to understand the whole wedding process to enable informed opinions on your part.

As the FOTB, you should stick your head in at the beginning of the planning for a few very good reasons. First of all, you are the secretary of the treasury. Traditionally, you are responsible for printing the bulk of the currency upon which the wedding will float. Though, quite often now, we see the engaged couple contributing financially to the budget (more on the funding models later). There will need to be an initial budget for discussion. All budgeting is again driven mainly by venue and the number of BIS—butts in seats. Humans consume food and alcohol, which is the largest cost.

What you want to do is try to provide some guidance and ask simple questions. Logic, not emotion, is what works now. According to The Knot, a wedding planning website, weddings currently cost over $28,000 on average in the US. This is not a trivial amount of money to spend, so the project needs to be done right.

As a major stakeholder in the funding process, all you are looking for is to gain comfort and confidence from a timeline and an understanding of:

• The key elements and vendors
• The key decisions and when they have to be made
• The costs and payment terms to help with cash flow

Who else is involved with planning? Well, your daughter might enlist some of her friends to help, but in a non-voting, non-spending role. Of course, the partner/groom and other members of the bridal party will be consulted. Additionally, the future parents-in-law will generally want to share thoughts on how the function should look and feel, since many of their friends and family will be making sacrifices of time and money to attend. The groom's family is also usually responsible for the rehearsal dinner. So, here is where a responsibility for the mother-in-law ties in to the overall master plan for timing and attendance.

A strong recommendation is to enlist the help of a wedding planner. They come in many different shapes and sizes. On one side of the spectrum is the full-service variety, who arranges everything, including managing all vendors. You just sit back, decide, and write checks. On the other side are the "day of" wedding planners. They are involved in deciding and recommending various segments of the wedding, but your family does most of the work until the wedding day. On that day, the "day-of" planner is on the ground, in charge of everything, so you just worry about getting dressed and getting to the ceremony on time.

Good planners are invaluable. They know the good and bad on the wedding front in your market. They know the ins and outs of all the venues, have contacts, understand how pricing works, and will be sensitive to your specific situation… big or small. Whatever path you take, the goal is to set up for a wedding day you can enjoy without worrying full-time about the flowers, the catering, and the entertainment.

FOTB Survival Tactic #3 – Enlist a planner if possible. A planner will soothe the FOTB's nerves with business-like dealings and experience in handling various aspects of the wedding.

Scene Two – Choosing the Venue

One of the very first decisions to make is where to hold your upcoming family event. Usually, there is some thought or preconception the team had in advance of the engagement. The venue will drive the number of attendees, timing, and of course… the cost. Deciding a venue has two large dimensions: geographic location and type of facility.

Where in the world will the wedding be held? Which city and why? Most weddings are held where the maximum number of family and friends invited can participate. Choices are the bride's home city, the groom's home city, or the couple's new home city, if different from other two. The wild card is opting for a destination wedding. That sound you hear in the background is a cash register going wild at the mention of the word "destination."

On the surface, holding the wedding in the bride's home city generally makes the preparations easier for the mother of the bride (MOTB), bride, and FOTB. Living in the same city as the site of the ceremony removes costs and presents fewer moving parts to be managed.

Ultimately, the geographic location of the wedding should be driven by taking a hard look at the probable pool of attendees. Without setting down a finite number of invitees, the team can take a view as to what may make sense if the thought is to veer from the default bride's home city location. If the bride's family is in the position of holding the purse strings, there is a definite weight to your opinion and direction on this topic.

Destination weddings are by nature more expensive. Fewer people may be willing to pay for flights and hotels to wedding destinations, whether it be coastal United States, Las Vegas, Hawaii or anywhere else in the world. Most likely some members of the family will be looking to the FOTB for a travel and food stipend to offset the cost. The attendance will not be the same type of number as one might have in a traditional setting back home.

It is an interesting fact that, according to The Knot, 80% of all destination weddings are for couples who have been married before. The most popular destinations in the continental US are Nevada, Florida, and California. Outside the US, the Caribbean, Mexico, and Hawaii are the most frequented for destination weddings.

However, if your budget is big enough and the family dream has always been a spectacular destination wedding, by all means, go for it. When you look at a destination wedding, you'll find most of the places you are considering have wedding packages and staff to plan, organize, and execute a wonderful wedding and reception. Most resort staff have far more experience than the "back home" wedding planners, due to the sheer volume of nuptials they manage. They've "been there" and "done that" with any and all possible scenarios involving far-flung incoming guests.

My second wife and I had a getaway wedding with just the two of us in Jamaica. Even though it was just us, the level of items to be arranged and handled by the resort team remained imposing. As we were checking in, the wedding coordinator took the bridal gown from my wife for safekeeping and managed us completely until the wedding was over. The resort team handled all the necessary paperwork work for our wedding license and certificate in a foreign country like a well-oiled machine, making everything easy for us.

Once you've landed on a geographic location for the wedding, the next question is, what type of venue: house of worship, hotel, country club, a home, or some type of specialized wedding facility such as a winery or farm? Since marriage is a high-volume business in America, you need a process to land on an answer quickly. To allow proper checking of availability, you should come up with a list of two or three candidates in a couple of different categories and prioritize them, as availability may knock some off your list. Venue and timing are partners in planning. Also, your initial thoughts on the number of invitees influences venue choices as well. It is very important to understand the minimum and maximum capacity of the prospective venues.

BUT WAIT. What about the reception? If your plan is a religious venue wedding, you most likely will need to find a separate site for the reception. This adds a level of complexity to the wedding day timeline, as the guests need to drive or be transported to the reception site, adding time to the length of the overall affair.

In summary, venue is the most time-sensitive element on the wedding project plan and must be tackled quickly. There is competition for many venues, and dates are commonly booked up to a year or more in advance. Figure out the type of venue, then get options and pricing from two or three places in two categories. Availability of your favored venue impacts timing for the wedding, so you can't plan too early.

FOTB Survival Tactic #4 – Having the ceremony and reception at the same site will reduce time, money, headache, and risks from the wedding day.

Scene Three – Timing

As mentioned earlier, the availability of a desired venue is an important part of the timing equation. Statistics show most engagements last over a year in duration. In fact, according to Wedding Wire, a wedding planning website, the average US engagement lasts fifteen months, so it's clear that most people planning a wedding are considering the time and venue they want well into the future.

Other than availability of a particular host site for the wedding and / or reception, what other factors weigh in the timing? The first factor is the weather. There's a reason so many brides want a May or June wedding: the weather is usually great, with good, consistent temperatures and predictable rain forecasts. The same is true for the fall months. Ask yourself, how many invitations have you ever gotten for a February wedding? With demand higher for weather-premium months, the task of finding a venue increases in importance.

Second, both families want maximum attendance. The planning team should review calendars to eliminate distraction or blocking weekends if you are considering a Friday night or Saturday ceremony.

Typical planning blockers include all children's end-of-year activities, especially graduations. Of course, this is a big consideration for May and June.

At the time of my daughter's wedding, we lived in Atlanta, Georgia and we were targeting a fall wedding. To ensure maximum attendance, we had to find a weekend on which both the University of Georgia and Georgia Tech were playing their football games away from home or had an off week. In all the southern states and most of the Midwest, particularly Ohio and Michigan, planning around fall college football is imperative.

Other potential blockers include known and sometimes unforeseen events such as medical procedures, service deployments, and other life events. You're not a fortune teller. Something is likely to happen in the months before the ceremony— trust me on that one.

Check all your information sources and create a workable list of wedding weekends to map against the availability of the potential venues. Be sure to loop in the in-laws, or serious ramifications could result. When you get a hit with a favored venue against a favored date, be prepared to pull the trigger and make the down payment. By that time, you should have a refined guest number for an accurate proposal and quote.

FOTB Survival Tactic #5 – Timing is the biggest factor in assuring maximum attendance. October, September, and June are the most popular months for weddings.

Scene Four – Number of Attendees

The key to how much the wedding costs is attendance. The Butts in Seat (BIS) number drives the size of venue and the food and drink requirements. Pretty basic cost accounting stuff. One to two hundred people watch your offspring get married and then you stuff them with food and booze.

The size of the guest list is an emotional minefield for the engaged couple's families... And don't forget the young couple's invitees. They will likely have a substantial number of friends, coworkers, and former classmates they may want at the wedding as well.

There is no really easy way to navigate building the initial guest list. A good way to start is to have everyone collect the names of their desired attendees on each side's family as well as the couple's own list. When you get those names, I suggest loading them into a spreadsheet, which will make the remaining steps easier. Now, examine the list of attendees through a couple of different lenses, the first being balance. Should the bride and groom have equal representation? Not all families have the same number of close family members and friends. It may be uncomfortable, but fair to do a review of every name and vet their importance to the ceremony. It is definitely optimal to have a large number of coworkers and bosses invited, if that is what the couple is comfortable with. Many of them are surrogate families for the bride and groom's families, with relationship bonds as close as many true family members.

I know it may seem a bit analytical, but for each person on the list, I suggest including a prediction as to whether they will attend. Also, enter the number of "pluses" for that invitation. In other words, are you going to invite a single person to bring a guest? Is a whole family invited, or just the two adults? This reflects the type and tone of wedding your family is putting together— formality versus familiarity, etc. Also, remember, increased BIS means an increase in dollars spent at the reception for food and drink.

The invitation list may be so large that a painful decision must be made to put some of the potential invitees into a B-list folder, where they are held until regrets start to come in. At that time, the B-list invitations are released and given the standard amount of time to respond.

One very interesting purpose of invitations came up during my daughter's wedding planning. Her future mother-in-law came from "society" in a small Georgia textile community. To her, the invitations were social announcements more than invitations. We had to send invitations out to a number of social scions who didn't know the groom from Adam but would recognize his mother's maiden name and family standing. The list included people such as the mayor of the city. Now, there was no way all these people were going to drive four hours from southern Georgia in November for our wedding. Nonetheless, we dutifully acquiesced and mailed these invitations southward. My wife, daughter, and I made an unspoken assumption that none of them were coming and went ahead and moved to the B-list of invitees.

The invitation list will be a source of trial and tribulation throughout the months. To avoid confusion, one person should manage the master list of invites sent, responses received, names of "pluses", and possible B-list invitation names. You will have to walk the line between generosity and ruthlessness with the guest list. It is appropriate to reach out to people and clarify their attendance as time approaches and seats get tight. Your goal is to get the maximum capacity you've budgeted and contracted for with people who truly want to be there and celebrate the day.

FOTB Survival Tactic #6 – Build and ruthlessly manage a list of invitees active, accepted, declined, and prospective. ONE person should own the master list or spreadsheet.

Scene Five – Out of Town Guest Accommodations / Hotel HQ for Wedding Day

Some percentage of your invited guests will be from out-of-town and will be expecting you to have secured a block of rooms at some hotel near the wedding venue. This should be arranged prior to sending the invitations out and form a part of the overall save-the-date communications and social media (I know, I haven't discussed save-the-date yet... I'll get there). The hotel will provide a code or some identifier for the guest to make a reservation securing a standard room at a discount.

There are a lot of advantages to having a "Ground Zero" or headquarters (HQ) for the wedding. First of all, it helps in getting the wedding party to the ceremony on time, especially the bridal party. With all of them in one place, you can marshal a minimum number of vehicles for transit to the ceremony. A successful wedding day is all about minimizing risk and the number of moving parts.

The best strategy is to book the hotel for two nights, the night of the rehearsal, and the night of the wedding.

Second, a central location provides an opportunity for family members and friends to connect before the wedding. It is a wonderful chance to meet the other side of the family. Usually, some great conversation and history can be gathered from these folks. I came away with very interesting and useful backstories from my HQ drinks with the in-law family.

It is very important that your arrangement with the hotel ensures room charges go to the guest and not you. In some situations, a card may be needed to hold a block of rooms. I have been involved in a personal instance where a relative convinced the front desk to put their charges on my card, and I didn't find out until the day after the wedding.

In some cases, the FOTB may understandably be picking up the room charges for some relatives or members of the wedding party. That is very generous, but you may want to make sure at the front desk that your generosity does not extend to the bar or restaurant. The wedding weekend is emotionally and financially draining enough without any additional surprises on your tab.

If your budget or frequent traveler points allow, you could consider upgrading your room to a suite, providing you comfort and space to entertain some of the guests and to host any impromptu emergency gatherings that may arise between the time of the rehearsal and the wedding ceremony.

FOTB Survival Tactic #7 – *As soon as the venue is set, arrange for a block of hotel rooms for the out-of-towners. Work on the invitation list should help determine the needed number. Communicate what costs YOU are picking up, if any, related to hotel charges.*

NOTE to DESTINATION WEDDING FOTBs: Accurate communication of the guest's responsible costs is important from the beginning and impacts accepting or declining invitations.

Scene Six – Budget Setting and Money Handling

It is very easy to fixate on the price of a wedding as one big lump sum. And realistically, it is the most important thing affecting the location, size, and atmosphere of the wedding. But I feel the FOTB should understand all the various elements a bit more before looking at the overall price tag.

Very possibly you've bandied about a number in your head for several years in fear of this blessed moment. Of course, just as when buying a house, a car, a boat, or anything else, the number is usually low. There is always something you didn't know or some additional features you "couldn't live without" that increase the end purchase price by five, ten or twenty percent.

While there are a whole lot of emotional pulls at you during the budgeting process, the FOTB must set a number he and his family are comfortable living with. Families pay for weddings in several different ways, including savings, credit, home equity loans, and money from the household budget. Some very smart parents—I haven't met too many— put money away over time for this event just as they would in saving for college. Always remember that the size and expense of a wedding does not guarantee marital success. Don't mortgage your future or incur debt that will saddle you down.

I have a close friend whose son was married at a large, beautiful church wedding with an expansive reception and a sit-down meal at a nearby hotel, including good liquor and a live band. There were probably two hundred people attending. This event was funded by the FOTB and easily cost him over $50,000. Well, the marriage lasted under a year. That's a tough pill no one wants to swallow, for sure.

Here is what average wedding expense costs were in 2022, according to the wedding planning website, The Knot:

- Venue $11,200
- Engagement Ring $5,600
- Live band $3,900
- Photographer $2,600
- Rehearsal dinner $2,400
- Florist $2,400
- Videographer $2,100
- Wedding dress $1,900
- Wedding planner $1,900
- DJ $1,500
- Transportation $980
- Invitations $510
- Cake $510
- Favors $440
- Groom's attire $290
- Hair and makeup $250
- Catering (per person) $75

Now, let's take a deeper dive into the major portions of the wedding budget.

> **FOTB Survival Tactic #8** – *The success and valued memory of a wedding is not based solely on the amount of money spent. Period.*

Wedding Dress

In looking at the list, there are items you should focus on and others that are not as important as you would think. First of all, let's talk about the dress. There is no limit to the amount of money that can be spent on a dress. And more isn't necessarily better.

The dress is going to be worn once for a handful of hours, cleaned, and likely put away— unless your daughter runs into the surf or jumps in a pool to trash the dress, which then really ends the useful life of that white asset. But usually, that's it!!! Finito!!! So the trick is to find a dress that makes your daughter look and feel beautiful.

Venue Rental

There are many considerations about the venue I have already high-lighted. As mentioned earlier, I am a huge proponent of a single location for both the ceremony and reception. It saves costs and transit time, with less contracts and staff to worry about. It's simpler.

I am fortunate to have a very smart daughter. She chose as her venue an old hotel, where a beautiful ballroom served as the location for both the ceremony and the reception. During the one-hour changeover interlude, the requisite pictures were taken at the front of the room while the aisles of chairs were repositioned for round dining tables. The floral arrangements were able to stay intact for the room as well.

The guests were invited into an area outside the ballroom, where a small bar had been set up for the short recess. They were also free to relax in other areas of the hotel, as well to pass the time during the break. This really did alleviate a lot of wear and tear on everyone.

Floral

Some thoughts about floral arrangements: a good plan is to utilize the ceremony arrangements for the reception as well. Of course, this is easy at the same physical venue. Invest enough in flowers to highlight the event and ensure the room doesn't feel like a cold conference room. But flowers are generally not what everyone remembers about a wedding. It is elegant and somewhat customary to have floral centerpieces on the tables that are available for some of the guests to take home.

Food and Beverage

Next on my hit list is the biggie: food and beverage. A couple of things to address out of the box. Do you want a sit-down meal, or a buffet line, and do you limit the type of alcohol? A sit-down meal costs about 20% more per guest than a buffet. If you are looking to have a greater air of formality or if the number of people at your reception precludes having a buffet line, then you've got a sit-down meal.

With regard to liquor, most families are limiting the available selection to beer and wines, and maybe some house-brand liquors. The wines will be a small, reasonable selection intended to cover the main red and white varieties. If a guest would like something different or top shelf, the guest would pay for the drink out of pocket.

If you serve alcohol at the wedding, just remember, it is meant to help enhance the event and evening, and not create its own event.

Entertainment

Another important item to consider is entertainment. Interestingly enough, this is the portion of the wedding celebration where I feel strong investment should be made. In my experience, the largest number of criticisms about any wedding are related to entertainment. Remember, everyone will be in the reception area for three or more hours together. One hour or so will be for speeches and setup, followed by dinner and music. So, most of the atmosphere outside of the ceremony is created by the entertainment you choose to provide.

The choices for entertainment are generally two: live performance with a small group, or a DJ playing recorded tunes. Either one works well, but only succeeds when there has been due consideration given to the type of audience and diversity of its members. The playlist(s) should be reviewed by the bride, the MOTB, and others to ensure there is a variety of songs that appeal to everyone at some point in the festivities. Depending on the age and the life stage of the guests, you will want to ensure there are songs and tempos appealing to all generations. Also, there should be enough songs included to allow slow dancing.

FOTB Survival Tactic #9 – Focus spending and attention on the venue and the entertainment. That's what will create the best memory for the attendees.

Photographer / Videographer

The next item on the list is the photographer / videographer. New technologies have brought great changes to the memorializing of the wedding since most FOTBs said "I do."

The digital and social media memorialization of weddings now often starts with a casual but loving photoshoot of the couple in a relaxed setting for the save-the-date announcement. Talk about something the photography and bridal industries made up for revenue! Unfortunately, it has become very much institutionalized and part of the wedding lifecycle. It's important that the FOTB be aware of this element and understand it when looking at bids for the entire video and photography package.

The cost drivers on videography are the number of photographers and amount of time you want them available to shoot pictures. The wedding day generally requires photography close to all day, to ensure capturing the intimate bridal preparation scenes and the bride's last moments with mom and dad as their single daughter. In addition to the requisite ceremony shots, the reception is a target-rich environment for great and also cringe-worthy shots of family and friends dancing after imbibing your free liquor.

Just like any other facet of the wedding, the sky is the limit on the photographer and videographer expense. Speaking of sky, many videographers are using drones for dramatic, overhead shots for "save-the-date" notices, the wedding ceremony, and the reception. It is impressive to see a video that starts at a distance and then flies up close to the couple and the festivities. The production will make your wedding look like an episode on HGTV, or an influencer's blog on YouTube.

As neat as all of this is, other than framing a few select pictures for family walls and tables, most of the video memories never really see the light of day much again. Other than during the first few weeks, or with other members of the wedding party, nobody is up for a trip through two hundred pictures and an hour or so of video.

So, be smart and efficient with the photo package choices. If you are helping to choose the photographer, try to look for someone who uses the scenery and background well for memorable shots. You know—those pictures that show emotion and really what the day is about. Anyone with a camera can order everyone to congregate for a group shot. It takes a special eye to catch the emotion and feeling of the moments creating the special character of the wedding day.

Money Handling

This topic has two key dimensions to it:

- Who is doing the funding?
- Who controls the outflow? Who writes the check or puts their credit card on the line?

With funding and handling there are usually three possibilities: parents, bride and groom, or hybrid. Similarly, there are the same choices for holding the money: parents, bride and groom, or hybrid.

When the parents fund and hold the money, the workings are pretty simple. The parents understand and agree on the budget and pay the bills as presented.

If the bride and groom totally fund the wedding, then they should and do manage the outflow to pay the bills along the way. Many couples who have been working for a few years and truly want to control the activity will push for this arrangement.

There are a couple of variations of the theme I have seen played out. The most notable is one in which the FOTB tells the couple he has a certain amount of money budgeted and available for the total wedding expense, which he puts into a joint checking account to which they have access. The kicker is that any money left after the wedding is theirs to keep. So, the FOTB writes one check and no more. The bride and groom ride herd over the budget and spending. And anything left at the end is money to help jumpstart their new life. I think this plan is brilliant, but I was too chicken to try it with my daughter. She should have signed me up for it, as she and her mother came in 10% under the number I had budgeted! I hope she doesn't read this and demand payment with interest.

In a hybrid funding model, both sets of parents bring a sum of money to the table, as do the couple. The monies can either be flung together in one pot, or each side can identify which parts of the budget they will be responsible for. The parents can also decide to simply split costs equally. Commonly, I have heard about the bride and groom wanting to amplify their event with a bigger sit-down dinner, or live entertainment with a several-piece band. So, the engaged couple uses their own money to provide something they know the parents might not be willing or able to afford.

Increasingly, no single party is paying for all of the expenses. According to the on-line wedding resource Zola, 16.6 percent of engaged couples are paying for the entire wedding, while 33.6 percent are paying for at least part of it. Parents or in-laws are paying for at least part of the wedding for 32.5 percent of couples, while 9.4 percent of parents or in-laws are bearing the cost for the entire wedding.

An important point to remember is that all the funding and handling models still require an agreed-upon budget. If you don't care about the budget and choose to hand your daughter a credit card with unlimited credit limit, I am not sure why you are reading this book!

Act Two: Event Preparation

Setting the Stage

Congratulations, FOTB! At this point in the drama, you have a plan and a budget, both of which are being tested on a daily basis. A date has been set and save-the-date notices are sticking on an average of 117 refrigerators across the country. The social media-savvy wedding teams have launched websites, Twitter feeds, Facebook pages, and other technology-driven attention-getters. As a FOTB, you should just stay out of the media stuff and let the wedding party do their thing.

Act Two is the longest portion of the wedding process. There is a combination of emotional, financial, and physical duress occurring during this period. I know you don't get to be fully in charge, but the role resembles General Eisenhower's when he was planning D-Day. Years of planning, thousands of men, and millions of dollars were used to build the hopefully successful formula for victory on June 6, 1944. However, all of it could be undone by the most trivial of things, such as a change in weather and miscommunications. What Ike relied on most to assuage his fears and risks was intelligence. He needed to know where the trouble spots were so he could plan an alternative or mitigate the risk.

As a FOTB, your patience, maturity, flexibility, and communication skills will be tested. You will be needed to listen to problems and contribute ideas for defusing common wedding issues between people when moments become heated. Let's take a look at the major activities in **Act Two.**

Scene One – Early Social Events

Once the engaged couple gets their feet under them and the world knows of the planned event, the social events will begin. The first known variety is an engagement party, which will often be hosted by the groom's family, or someone in the nexus of the couple's social circle.

The second type of social event is the wedding shower. For the sake of simplicity, I am including under this heading the notion of teas, luncheons, and other celebratory functions. There are a lot of potential emotional pain points around wedding showers. It is all about who gets credit for planning and putting on the event, and who gets to be involved.

When the bride shares her joyous news of engagement to Mr. Perfect, the first thing out of some people's mouths will be, "Ooooh… I want to hold a shower for you." This is one of those freeze-frame moments and areas where men are completely different from women. Men never volunteer for responsibility over something like this. We might offer to help or bring something, but definitely not to take the captain's chair on the SS Bridal Shower.

Wedding showers or related entertainments such as couples' showers can be family-member-led or friend-led. Quite often, both mothers will hold a shower for the bride-to-be.

If there is only one family-led shower, there is potential for a flashpoint to be navigated as to who will lead. Without being overly dramatic, I want to point out that the issue of showers is full of possible power plays and angst between the MOTB and MOTG (mother of the groom). A diplomatic sense of fair play and sharing between the two mothers will need to occur. At this point, these women are setting the stage and establishing turf that will extend into the longer relationship between the two. The best choice for arbiter in this potentially touchy area is the bride, because the event is for her, and she should have a majority vote in the direction of the shower. There are plenty of roles, tasks, and assignments the bridal shower organizer can hand out to placate the masses. It is much like a new president appointing ambassadors around the globe—a lot of credit but not necessarily a whole lot of work to get it.

The FOTB should try to participate and support the MOTB and bride as best possible. Feathers might be ruffled, but hopefully no wings will be broken. One more thing for the FOTB to remember is that women tend to have a longer memory than men (I know I didn't really need to point that out). So, the smallest issue will continue to burn bright for months. And, we still have a long way to go until the ceremony day.

Some people choose to honor the engaged couple with a couples' shower. The primary difference here is that spouses and partners are invited along with the women who would usually attend a wedding shower, but this is much different than an engagement party. The invited parties bring a shower gift, which most likely will be in addition to the actual wedding gift. Alcohol may be present, but this is not a party kind of vibe, so everyone should keep the atmosphere under control.

The FOTB should focus on talking and connecting with the bridal party members plus their partners, whom he may not already know. When I have attended couples' showers, I gained a greater sense from their friends of who the bride and groom really were as adults. A couple's parents may have a hard time seeing their children through a lens that isn't colored by their childhood, and chatting with the young couples' school friends and work colleagues offers them a new perspective on their adult children.

FOTB Survival Tactic #10 – *Enjoy the parties and showers. Participate, empathize with MOTB, and be a gracious FOTB.*

Scene Two – Bridal Gown and Other Threads

I must admit I had nothing to do with picking out my daughter's gown. And unlike all the reality bridal shows on cable, I haven't met an FOTB who went to the various shops for dress showings and fittings. I DO know that it is a very good idea to sample quite a few and pare the selection down for iterative review. A few days distance between viewings can truly alter an opinion formed after the first showing... It's very interesting how that works.

The bridal gown is another early and expensive budget item. It is purchased relatively early, and the production and alterations can take quite a while to get done. About three months should be budgeted to be conservative for this.

The average bridal gown in the US costs $1,600 dollars with alterations. According to online wedding resource The Knot, most spend under $2,000, with 25% coming in between $2,000 and $3,000, and 10% spending over $3,000. It can be a big range. Where you land in that range is completely up to how your daughter wants to look and feel on the wedding day. Some want simple and elegant, and other women want to be princesses with a fancier gown.

Many brides realize saving on the dress will provide additional budget for other parts of the wedding, such as the venue and the entertainment.

The good news is that the decision of which gown will be selected is often supported by input from several friends and family, who will go along to the dress selection sessions that are scheduled with the boutiques. The Knot advises that most brides try on four to seven dresses before landing on "the one." The consensus tends to land at the right place, but the bride knows in which dress she feels most comfortable and beautiful; in which she feels most like a bride.

With the bridal gown selection put to bed for a several months' sleep, there are still other clothing landmines. Coordination between the MOTB and MOTG must occur regarding color and style of dresses they are wearing. The worst thing in the world is for the two mothers to have a *wardrobe collision* and look alike or similar on the wedding day.

There are a couple of other commandments for the MOTB and MOTG dresses:

- Do not outshine the bride. The dress should not look close in style to a wedding dress or bridal party dress.
- Mothers should look like mothers. Dresses should look like something an adult would wear.
- Resist anything tight-fitting advertising recent surgical enhancements performed or Pilates mastery.

Let's turn the page from gowns and dresses to men's apparel. First of all, let's get one thing straight... you, as the FOTB, really have no choice in the matter. The bride will drive the choice of apparel; tuxedo, suit, kilt, loincloth, or whatever her vision for the day dictates.

As the interested party with no direct influence in the decision, all you can do is trust your daughter to choose the apparel that will look best and suit the season and venue. One thing all should consider is that collapsing with a heat stroke during the ceremony may look good on America's Funniest Home Videos, but not on the video you're buying, or the livestream on Facebook. Finding some way to minimize the layers and heaviness of the suit or tuxedo will be appreciated by all. This is especially true in an outdoor or resort setting for the ceremony. Men sweat, and men about to get married really sweat. And men carrying too much extra tonnage standing in a wedding ceremony really, really sweat.

When my sister was married, I was a groomsman and we had to take a hand towel with us into the church for the groom. It was June in Georgia, and the ceremony was a Catholic high mass, which for non-Catholic readers means an hour-long service. It was torture for all of us, but mostly for my poor brother-in-law, who drenched his tuxedo.

The other bridal party members to consider are the young ones: ring bearers, flower girls, and other associated wee ones appointed to come down the aisle as well. They will be kitted out in miniature versions of bridesmaid and groomsman apparel. One word of warning is to consider how many months there are between the clothing order date and the wedding. Children grow, and there are very few options on the day before or of a wedding to alter the outfits.

FOTB Survival Tactic #11 – *Don't be afraid to put a budget on the wedding dress but be prepared to go up a few percentage points for the PERFECT dress.*

Scene Three – Attendance Management

In **Act One**, your team successfully managed to overcome familial, emotional, geopolitical, and fiscal barriers to create a workable pool of invitees with an agreed-upon attendance number. With that being done, one member of the team was asked to be responsible for the creation of the invitations. The MOTB and bride normally are in charge of addressing the invitations, which is no small task. And for some, if you are going old school, it may need to be outsourced due to lack of good penmanship.

Standard protocol dictates invitations should be sent six to eight weeks before the ceremony, with an expected response within four weeks— generally one month prior to wedding. If you can get all the invitations ready for a big drop on the outside allowable date, that is great. Otherwise, a suggestion is to ensure sending the invitations for those guests thought most likely to send regrets. An additional suggestion is to send the first batch of invites to the out-of-towners (or at least those you really expect to come) so you can get a handle on what kind of hotel and transport arrangements need to be made.

As soon as a regret is received, an invitation should be sent to someone from your B-list, if your team has determined you need one. The RSVPs must be managed constantly and ruthlessly to appease both sides of the aisle. It is advisable to keep up constant contact and flow of information to the bride and the MOTG on the RSVP status.

It is normal to plan for about a 75 – 85 percent acceptance rate. That percentage can be affected by the number of in-town invitees. In other words, if your list is heavily weighted with in-towners, they have a higher acceptance rate, right? They have less of a barrier to attendance since there are no travel costs. The reason this percentage is important is that some will make an A-List of invitees that is greater than the seating capacity, assuming a certain number will send regrets.

The save-the-date communication that occurred six to eight months before the wedding date helps people plan, driving a higher acceptance rate. Many will communicate in advance of the actual invitation their attendance intentions, which greatly aids in understanding where the attendance number stands.

As FOTB, you will need to be a polite jerk at times. There will be a period when it looks like there will be more attendees than seats. If you really need to up the attendance, reach out through your planner to negotiate a new block size for the wedding.

FOTB Survival Tactic #12 – Perform several iterations of the invitation list between the save-the-date release and the invitation send date.

Scene Four – Cakes, Food, and Alcohol

For the FOTB, there are few activities that are just fun and don't have any emotional landmines or traps associated with them. The cake and food tasting is one of them. The tastings are organized affairs where some portion of the wedding party will go along with bride and groom to a bakery or upscale market to taste slices of a set of prearranged cake choices.

When eating the sample pieces— and yes, sometimes you get to take some home with you— there are no wrong answers. Just tell the cake people what you think, what you like, and why. It's easy, mainly because you can say whatever you want, as your opinion is like a mail-in vote in the elections and gets counted only if the election results are really close.

Now, you may have some family members who are great cooks and can bake really great cakes and have the nth generation secret recipe for wedding cake and icing. Inevitably, they may volunteer to make the cake. It is fantastic that they care this much and want to help. However, if they're really not in the business of making cakes for weddings, the risk factor is high. There are a lot of considerations involving the cake, in addition to just baking and icing. The pros have special equipment, vehicles, and techniques to transport, assemble, and repair a multi-tier wedding cake.

A very successful strategy is to placate the volunteering relatives by asking them to handle a secondary cake, such as the groom's cake, if you are planning to have one at the reception. There is a lot less risk and moving parts with those cakes. By its nature, the groom's cake is easier to transport and assemble on-site. Most importantly, it is not the centerpiece for key reception activities and video memorializing. This is a win-win for the FOTB and MOTB.

You made your choice months ago about having a buffet or sit-down dinner at the reception. There is really nothing to do now, as you are locked into a few menu choices for sit-down dinners: beef, chicken, seafood, or vegetarian. And the buffet you signed up for will have those choices. All venues should be able to cater to vegetarian, ethnic cuisines, and other special needs. As part of the venue selection, most brides and grooms have a taste test of the proposed menu. There are many questions to ask during the tasting (see appendix), but two key ones are: who is cooking the food we are tasting right now, and how far the kitchen is from the reception room?

With the first question, you want to find out if the venue is stacking the cards and using their best chef to bait the hook. With the second, the desire is to minimize distance from kitchen to table and maximize freshness and taste.

A key suggestion regarding the food and drink is to stick with the plan. This is the major driver in the wedding costs and really should not be mucked with at the eleventh hour.

I almost forgot about alcoholic beverages. Remember, FOTB, when it comes to liquor at your signature family event, you should be focused on not on getting everyone drunk, but on letting them drink enough to relax and enjoy the festivities.

A quick story about liquor at weddings. A business friend of mine had a nice Catholic church wedding followed by a country club reception. While the post-ceremony pictures were being taken, he got a cell phone call from the bar at the country club. The word was that the $5,000 worth of liquor bought for the event was running out. It was a Sunday and places to get boxes of liquor were limited, if not zero. Miraculously, additional supplies were found, and the wedding party had to pick up cartons of liquor bottles on the way from the church to the reception. As he described it, the scene upon entering the reception was a mad house, with lots of old folks at the bar being served two or three drinks at a time.

In summary, the best practice is to limit alcohol to pre-selected beer and wine. If the guests don't like it and want something else, try to have a cash bar option if possible. Again, the day is not supposed to be about drinking.

FOTB Survival Tactic #13 – The food and beverages are important in setting the best possible atmosphere for the reception. Guests may remember the liquor options more than the food options. Work hard to stay within your budget.

Scene Five – Emotional Rescue

The hardest part of **Act Two** is the calendar length of time it occupies. After the initial burst of connecting, planning, and deciding, the main participants in our event settle into a daily routine. As in the movie "Groundhog Day," every morning when you hit the alarm button, the ever-present image of the wedding looms in your mind. It is the major —and sometimes only— topic of family discussions. Most every week has some deadline, activity, or action everyone must be involved in. The pressure can seem a bit unrelenting and daunting.

The tenor of the relationship of the engaged couple changes from "romance and roses" to one of burden and pressure around the wedding planning. The groom may feel as if he has lost his woman to another entity: the wedding. With pressure naturally come short tempers or blow-ups. Married couples might have a good argument every six to nine months without the pressure of a wedding bearing down on them.

So every engagement will likely face a couple of major blowups stemming from the most innocent and innocuous of items or comments. Some of these will mature into full-fledged breakups, where one or the other partner is questioning whether they should be spending the rest of their lives together.

Anyway, the FOTB and MOTB are there to counsel and console their daughter. Assure her that her fiancé does love her, and every good partnership encounters bumps in the road. Let her know they can and will work out these differences.

If needed and asked for by the fiancé, the FOTB should be willing to coach the future son-in-law into apologizing —always a good start—and share insights about his daughter. Let the groom know how much she loves him and how all marriages need to learn how to manage through the emotional storms.

Hopefully both will quickly come to their senses and keep the wedding train moving. Please note I am not delving into areas where either of the couple has committed some capital offense that truly breaches the trust of the other.

Just as Mick Jagger sings, you'll likely come to their "emotional rescue" at least once before the ceremony.

***FOTB Survival Tactic #14** – Most engagements are 15 months long. Try to schedule breaks away from the wedding planning, especially for FOTB and MOTB.*

Scene Six – Get in Shape

Try to mentally project yourself forward in time ten or maybe twenty years from now. You are standing in your daughter's living room and hanging on the wall are several pictures from her wedding. Of course, we have our fingers crossed and pray that the couple are still together that long.

As you gaze at the pictures, only one thought hits you as you look at the picture for the thousandth time. "Geez, I look like crap. I look like a whale."

Do you want that? At a minimum, do you want to have to wear men's Spanx —there is such an offering—underneath your tuxedo or suit? I can tell you from personal experience, you do not want to add more clothing on a day when your blood pressure will be up already.

The answer is simple: get in shape. I think most FOTBs can stand to drop a few pounds. You want to look good in the pictures, which will be revered for decades. And you want to look good on the dance floor with your daughter.

If your wife shares your desire to look her best for the wedding, perhaps you can set goals, work together, and hold each other accountable in a weight-loss program. Really work hard the last sixty to ninety days before the ceremony. The only potential downside is that your tuxedo or the MOTB's dress may have to be altered to accommodate the new you. Is that such a bad thing? Sounds like a triumphant moment and a badge of honor to me.

> *FOTB Survival Tactic #15 – Get in freakin' shape!*
> *Avoid the men's Spanx.*

Scene Seven - Late Social Events

You are in the homestretch of the FOTB Wedding Derby when the bridal party and the groom's party have their celebrations. These can range from a simple dinner and gathering to more elaborate away time. Like most every facet of a wedding, the expanse of these events can vary.

I think we're familiar with the TV and movie version of bridal parties that feature a trip away for one or two nights, usually somewhere with a spa and plenty of wine. The program is to wear nice robes, watch chick flicks, spa a lot, and drink wine. This is not to be confused with a party just before the wedding, where the bride-to-be wears a banner and tiara on a party bus traversing many bars, with possible stops at strip clubs featuring large-chested and otherwise well-endowed men providing evocative dance and party favors. Not all brides relish or agree to these activities, but they do make for good stories and movie fodder.

If the groomsmen have organized a celebratory gathering, it is generally not as steeped in tradition as the women's events. The groomsmen are more apt to declare a ski weekend or find a city to see a concert and crash some brew pubs. Regardless, it will most likely be quite different than the women's weekend.

The good news for you, Mr. FOTB, is that you are not usually involved in these events. Kick back and enjoy some peace and quiet because the big day is around the corner.

FOTB Survival Tactic #16 – *Enjoy the weekend; it is the quiet before the storm.*

Act Three: The Wedding

Setting the Stage

And then suddenly, the calendar page turns, you rub your eyes, and it is the week of the wedding. Congratulations! You and the team have mobilized at least two families, possibly one to two hundred quests, tuxedos, dresses, floral arrangements, and a venue that will all hopefully come together as a wonderful symphony for your daughter.

This is *the* week of ultimate worry and much-needed flexibility. If you have a day-of planner, they check all the arrangements for the venue and supporting vendors. There is an amazing number of smallish errands, pick-ups, and gotchas to be handled most all week, but they culminate on the day of the rehearsal. That is the day most men go to pick up their tuxedos. Some of the groomsmen might be from out of town and arrive just a few hours before the rehearsal. In some situations, you may have to pick up several tuxedos and pray they fit the groomsmen.

I would advise the FOTB not to travel for business that week. Stay in town and be available. And take the day of the rehearsal off, as well as the day before, if possible. Your wife will love you for it. Your role that week is to be executive go-fer and take as much off your wife and daughter's shoulders as possible.

Just like a holiday, you have a house to stock with food and liquor for family coming in before and hanging about after the wedding. You may also be taking some food and beverage to the wedding HQ hotel that will need prep and travel.

Communication with the in-laws about the rehearsal dinner will be on tap for FOTB and MOTB. This is generally their show to set up and run, but it must flow in concert timewise with the wedding rehearsal. Revalidation and alignment on timings for the rehearsal day are needed early and often during the final week.

One of the most important items on the list for the FOTB to perform in the final week is to finish preparations and practice the FOTB speech. More on this to come, but this is a big deal, and you want to get it right.

The FOTB executive taxi and limo service may be activated to retrieve family members from the airport. Plan well ahead, as this can eat up a lot of valuable time at the end of the week.

I suggest FOTBs review the attendee list and try to gain some intel on key attendees. It's also important to find out about any potential landmines or family traps you want to avoid in conversation.

Finally, get the cash and tip envelopes ready. Your planner will give you guidance as to what is best. You probably thought the contract amount was your only obligation on the wedding day. But no. You will think you're a mob boss paying off politicians by the time you're finished after the reception.

FOTB Survival Tactic #17 – *Make yourself as available as possible during the wedding week. Your week will fill up quickly.*

Scene One – Rehearsal

Rehearsals and rehearsal dinners are usually held the day or night before the actual ceremony. This is a time that is an absolute convergence of nerves and emotions.

The team that has been driving the wedding plans —parents, bride, groom, and planners— have all the arrangements about the event swirling around in their heads and stomachs... worrying about the catering, the flowers, entertainment, seating, and so on. There are a whole lot of worst-case scenarios being imagined on the day before.

While the rehearsal is meant to be a light and practical run-through of the ceremony, it is interesting how real everything can suddenly become. The practice can end up being an emotional catharsis for some of the participants, who've been steeped in the wedding journey for ALL the months since your daughter said yes to your future son-in-law.

Quick story on this point: at my daughter's rehearsal, she and I stood back in the lobby while the minister set all the other players in place at the front. The entry procession was rehearsed nicely, and then it was time for me to practice walking the bride down the aisle. The aisle was a couple of hundred feet from the altar, so the distance did look a bit imposing. But when I held my daughter's arm and gently said, "let's practice walking—slowly and gracefully— as all eyes will be on you," the floodgates opened, and she burst into tears. The room went silent as she sobbed while we walked ever so slowly down the aisle.

My future —and still current— son-in-law smiled, looked at us and offered up to his bride-to-be a truly inspired question: "Those are tears of joy, right?" Everyone started to laugh and got through the emotions of the moment. The tears were clearly a relief and release of everything she'd been through to get to that day. It was a scene fitting for any great romantic comedy on TV.

The rehearsal is what it says it is; just a rehearsal and not the real deal. So, the FOTB hasn't really faced the truth about losing his daughter yet. But the clock is ticking, and he has about twenty-four hours.

My general belief is that the whole rehearsal day is a bit of an ordeal. First, there is all the activity and errands that have gone on during the day. Second, depending on your location, the wedding party may have to endure rush-hour traffic on a weekday afternoon to get to the venue for the rehearsal. My personal experience was the great fun of navigating downtown Atlanta traffic on a Friday afternoon.

FOTB Survival Tactic #18 – Try hard to relax. There is already a high amount of stress in the system. Enjoy the trial walk with your daughter down the aisle.

Scene Two – Rehearsal Dinner

But wait, there's more... you must get the wedding party from the venue to the site of the rehearsal dinner, which is NOT ever going to be convenient to the venue. I think that is a rule in one of the bridal magazines.

It seems that the traditions and wedding calendars are intended to wear everyone down to the nub before the wedding day. If it was up to me, there would be a spa day and/or a golf day between these two events.

So now it is early evening, and you are heading to the rehearsal dinner. These can occur in all sizes and shapes, varying from small to large in attendance and buffets to lavish sit-down affairs. This is an occasion where the in-laws can make a statement, should they choose to, since they're generally not responsible for a majority of the wedding's financial obligations. On average, rehearsal dinners cost about $1500.

I have never understood the formula and logic for attendees at the rehearsal dinner. I think the origin of the event was to provide dinner for the wedding party and out-of-town guests. But now, the attendance formula is hard to pin down and often includes lots of people who are "just like family."

My son was married once, and his bride-to-be inflated the rehearsal dinner invitee list to include people "just like family," whom she'd stated just weeks earlier that she hugely disliked and didn't want at the wedding. The irony was strong, but I still had to pick up the check.

As I mentioned earlier, my son-in-law's mother was from an upper-class social setting and upbringing in south Georgia. The rehearsal dinner she produced was an amazing affair at a nice private club with a sit-down dinner and open bar. There were probably close to ninety people in attendance. It even included a video montage of pictures chronicling the lives of the bride and groom before and after they met. I must admit it was emotional to see those pictures taking us all the way back to when we first brought the bride-to-be home from the hospital.

As the FOTB, the cautionary word is to drink lightly, if at all. You want to make a good impression on all the people you meet for the first time at this event. And you've got the real match left to play the next day.

One major piece of advice is to always be prepared to make some sort of remark. You may not be called upon but have a story or something nice ready to say about the groom and how much he will mean as part of your family. At my daughter and son-in-law's rehearsal dinner, there was a microphone and speaker system available for the audience to share stories and generally embarrassing tales about the bride and groom.

As I was sitting at the table with the groom's parents, the MOTG looked at me and said, "Mike, you're a pretty good speaker; why don't you say a few words?" I took a long sip of my *one* gin and tonic and stood up in front ninety people, over half of whom I had never met.

During the pre-dinner festivities, I had the opportunity to meet my son-in-law's grandfather, a grand gentleman retired from practicing law in Augusta, Georgia. I learned from him of a family tradition in which he had a brick inscribed for every family member and positioned in a large walkway in his backyard. So, as you married or were born into the family, your name appeared inscribed on a brick in his walkway. I found this to be one of the warmest family traditions I'd ever heard of.

With microphone in hand, I looked around the room, and bought some time by reintroducing myself and saying how excited we were to meet the in-law's family and have William as part of our world. Then inspiration struck and said, "I just learned tonight from Paw-Paw about the wonderful brick tradition you have at the family home in Augusta. I have to say I am moved and touched by that… it is amazing."

I then continued and addressed William's grandfather. "Now, Paw-Paw, I do have just one question. I know you install a brick when someone marries in, but what happens if…"

I didn't have a chance to finish the sentence hinting at a marital demise before a deep, regal Southern voice boomed throughout the whole room, "Well son, those bricks aren't in cement…" The house came down in laughter, and you'd have thought Paw-Paw and I had rehearsed that line for a month. And by the way, there is a recorded family "brick-ectomy" in Paw-Paw's walkway.

My point is for the FOTBs to be ready; to enjoy the new friends and family, learn about them and appreciate who they are. These few days of wedding festivities form the honeymoon in the relationship between the two families, and everyone should be in the best of spirits, wanting the entire event to be a success, so take advantage of building on these warm feelings.

After the rehearsal dinner you and MOTB will retire either to your home —with possible guests— or the HQ Hotel. Staying at a hotel is another opportunity to catch up with old friends, family, and new family before the big day. The rest of the day and evening should be low-key and stress-free prior to the big day.

There may be late-night festivities, especially among the male members of the bridal party, that you definitely don't want to know about. As you coast off to a well-earned sleep, your day-ending thought might be a prayer that the groom gets to the venue the next day and he's not re-enacting a re-do of the movie "The Hangover" with Bradley Cooper and posse.

FOTB Survival Tactic #19 – Enjoy the evening and be prepared to address the crowd with something focused on the groom and his family.

Scene Three - Wedding Day

Wake up FOTB, the day is finally here. If you are fortunate to have engaged a wedding planner, they have scripted out the timeline for everyone as to when and where to be, and what to be dressed in.

If you have an evening wedding, the morning seems snail-like, just waiting for it to be time for something to happen. Some grooms' parties will play nine holes of golf and have lunch to kill the time. Just keep any imbibing under control. You want to avoid having a drunken groom or groomsmen.

Otherwise, you will probably have breakfast with friends or family to catch up; a lot of that goes on, and that's what weddings are for. One thing that it is important to do first thing if you didn't do it after the rehearsal dinner is to inventory your wardrobe. Make sure you've got the tux or suit and all the accessories required. It is easy to forget socks and cuff links.

Luckily, you do not have a starring role in the hair and makeup activities for the bridal party. Those poor ladies have a lo-o-o-ong day, but it is usually cushioned by a nice assortment of sandwiches, cheese, fruit, and of course, wine. At my daughter's wedding, I did pop in to say hello and see a bit of what the money was paying for. I am always amazed at what the bridal make-up and hair specialists accomplish in a few hours. Also, they must be part therapist and psychologist to deal with all the emotions they're exposed to for four to five hours.

Hopefully you took care of it on a day when the banks were open, but you will need cash and envelopes. You and the MOTB need to sit down and go through the list and number of servers and people who should be tipped. You may also have been advised about a suggested formula for the tip. All the wait staff and bar staff should be tipped. I don't remember the exact amount, but I did have a pile of twenty- and hundred-dollar bills going into many envelopes. Put the money somewhere very secure, as you won't hand it out until the reception is nearly finished.

I keep bringing up the concept of the planner, but if you've got one... life is good. They are running the show and all the anxiety should be on their shoulders. Wedding day planning is definitely a good thing to have outsourced... trust me.

Even with a great planner and a timeline, anxiety creeps in and your blood pressure goes up. It's natural. If you have something or need to take something to relax you a bit, do so. The higher demand for possible pharmaceuticals will be in the bridal room. Relaxation is good, but care should be taken to avoid any over-relaxed scenes like the bride in the movie "Sixteen Candles," who took enough muscle relaxants to knock out Secretariat.

With all the stress and emotions involved today, not everyone will be thinking straight. Another part of your role as FOTB is to provide an air of calm and ensure there are as few moving parts as possible. This is especially true in transportation logistics. Fewer vehicles and drivers is the best strategy. You also want to have as much buffer time as possible built into the timeline to allow for the unexpected to occur... which it will.

Oh yeah, I almost forgot: keep track of the old people. The elderly guests require more corralling and shepherding. And time is a whole different concept to them. You must manage the grandparents; they will wander off on you if you don't keep up with them.

Probably the most important task for the day is, as the old saying goes, "get them to the church on time." As FOTB, you have no dominion over the groom's party, but the bride's group is your responsibility. Don't wait till the last minute to figure out how many vehicles are going and who's going in which one. And for the sake of all that's holy, don't let an out-of-towner have any key driving roles. Even with GPS on our phones, try not to leave things to chance.

My daughter's maid-of-honor was from south Georgia—that seems to be a recurring theme in my stories. Even though she went to Georgia Tech, she had no sense of direction or idea of Atlanta traffic. As we were herding the bridal party into a couple of vehicles for the drive to the venue, she declared she would drive herself from the hotel as a bit of a sightseeing trip. That was a bad idea. Images of the maid-of-honor lost, and circling Atlanta were spinning in my mind. I gently but firmly grasped her shoulders and guided her into the back of my wife's car, suggesting she could do her sightseeing the next day.

A final thought: I hope you did get into a diet program months earlier as suggested if it was necessary. Otherwise, you probably went on-line and ordered some men's Spanx. Possibly the T-shirt and underwear combination. If you're wearing it, you've added time to your bathroom visits and about ten degrees of body heat underneath the tux, shirt, and possibly a vest.

FOTB Survival Tactic #20 – *Follow the plan, timeline, and checklist for the wedding day. This is not a good day to ad-lib and go off the script.*

Scene Four – Wedding Ceremony

Good job! Everyone is now at the venue, you hope. Your planner, if you have one, has gotten the flowers into their proper places and the venue looks great.

For you FOTBs who went all out with a destination, hopefully your setting looks spectacular, and the weather is cooperating with you.

In all situations, it's another hurry-up-and-wait. You get to the venue one to two hours ahead of time to wait. The posted arrival time gives enough buffer to allow people to be lost and late but still fit within the desired window.

Once at the venue for the ceremony, part of the FOTB's role is to lead by example and get some food and drink into people. Without any sustenance in their systems, everyone is a good candidate for passing out during the wedding ceremony.

The wedding ceremony is a target-rich environment for possible YouTube and America's Funniest Home Video moments. We've all enjoyed watching wedding accidents and disasters on TV. We just don't want millions to laugh at us if we can help it. Here are some risks you will have hopefully taken into account in planning the ceremony:

- **Fainting.** The combination of nerves, emotions, lack of food, and heat from the gowns and / or tuxedos can knock down many a wedding party member. Men will tend to lock their knees while standing, which any soldier knows will hasten a faint.
- **Candles.** Lighting of candles, walking with candles, or any sort of flame near a bridal gown or veil is risky. There are many videos of veils going up like a haystack on fire.
- **Water and water features.** This is more of a concern for outdoor settings, where the path to the altar may go across a bridge or next to a pond or water feature. It is very easy for one of the wedding party to lose focus or balance for a split second and end up in the drink.
- **Tripping and falling in general.** Women are often wearing long dresses for the first time, in addition to high heels. They are coached to walk slowly down the aisle, not just for the drama of the moment but also to help keep them from tripping on the dress. Steps up to the appointed position at the altar can provide a challenge to the ladies in long dresses and new shoes, which are smooth and slippery. It is tempting to look up at the rest of the party and take your eye off the ball going up a step or two. The rehearsal hopefully will have given everyone a good sense of the terrain.

Okay. With all the possible ceremony YouTube moments out of the way, let's focus on the event that starts the wedding ceremony: the walk with your daughter down the aisle. This walk is a symbolic and physical transition in life. Your daughter goes down the aisle unmarried and a central part of your immediate family. When she walks back in a short while, she will be married. Still your daughter, but her primary role in life will now be as a wife, partner, and possible parent. All things change at the end of that walk.

If you have been thinking up and saving some loving words of care and reassurance for your daughter, this is the time to say them. Remind the bride to enjoy the moment and savor it with a regal walk down the aisle. I am still struck by the memory of the smiles and joy I witnessed on the guests' faces during those momentous minutes. It was truly moving and made everything feel worthwhile.

I don't know if it gets any easier with a second or third bride, but it was very hard to walk my daughter down the aisle. From the wedding pictures, I can tell my face was flushed and my blood pressure was probably up a few points.

After the handing over of your daughter to her very soon-to-be husband, you take your place of honor beside the MOTB. If you are lucky, your MOTB will offer a loving glance, smile, or pat on the thigh to basically say, "good job!", thanking you for all efforts as a father in raising the bride and supporting the wedding. For me, the rest of the ceremony was a blur as I reflected on the years and memories making up who my daughter had become.

And in a blink of an eye, you hear the officiant pronounce the couple man and wife, watch the kiss, and hear the recessional music begin.

Most of the time between the ceremony and the reception is often taken up with pictures and possibly transit to the reception site if it is a different location.

FOTB Survival Tactic #21 – Avoid the YouTube moments and savor the walk... don't rush it.

Scene Five – Wedding Reception

With the huge emotional pressure of the wedding ceremony off your shoulders, you'll now enter the longest period of the event. I know you're tired, exhausted, and emotionally spent, not just from the wedding day, but from the accumulation of wear and tear over the months leading up to it.

Sort of like the Ironman Triathlon, the reception is the marathon part of the day's festivities. You're tired, but you're staring at another four to five hours before you hit the real finish line. There are a couple more spotlight activities for the FOTB before he can relax a bit.

The reception can begin a couple of ways. The first is for guests to be settled in their seats with an adult beverage in hand before the new husband and wife are announced and make their way through the room to the designated wedding party table.

Alternatively, there may be a receiving line for the guests to meet the key members of the wedding party as they enter the reception area. A receiving line was commonplace "back in the day," and is still often used at large weddings. I understand the pros and cons of a receiving line. The wedding party does get a chance to greet everyone, which may not be the case once all are seated. With a crowd of over one hundred, the small amount of time available to circulate the entire room can be rather daunting.

However, the entry to the reception is set up, it is important for FOTB and MOTB to greet everyone, make contact, and thank them for coming to the wedding. It is also a duty of the bride and groom to work the room and thank everyone for making the time to participate in their wedding celebration. Take it from personal experience— the bride and groom will score huge points if they can circulate through the room like politicians, greeting, smiling, offering a bit of banter, and then moving on. My son-in-law was taught good social graces by his mother, and you would have thought he was running for governor the way he made his way through a room crowded with 150 people. I am not sure my daughter had smiled as much in her life as she did during the reception.

At this point, the FOTB has two major duties. One is to serve as an ambassador for the family and overall wedding, dispensing goodwill and ensuring everyone has a good time. The second is to be a marshal. As a marshal, you need to keep everyone behaving and safe. Don't let people take too much advantage of your free alcohol and spoil the happy day. You probably know who the strongest candidates are for celebration abuse, so keep an eye out for them.

As we talked about earlier in the wedding day, be sure to eat something. Alcohol and fatigue can sweep over the best of us, especially with no food in the stomach. Also, if you have a chance to lose the Spanx... do so now. Wearing them for up to twelve hours gets a bit old and bothersome. Ditch them as soon as you can after the wedding pictures are taken. You will enjoy the rest of the evening much more without the man corset on.

At the reception, all the magic video moments tend to come from dancing. The wonderful shots of guests falling and tripping stem from the three big things that affect someone's balance: alcohol, age, and weight. How come at a wedding, people who normally can't even walk to the car without pain decide to relive Saturday Night Fever and chase John Travolta onto the dance floor? You won't be able to talk common sense to all your senior or high-risk guests but be ready.

Above all, do not let anyone climb on the tables to dance. Aside from being a probable million-hit YouTube moment, a guest is guaranteed to get injured because of the flimsiness of the dining tables. Keep your older guests under control.

If your team and the planner have done everything right and been lucky, the reception will be a great affair and enjoyed by all. But before you can turn the guests loose to the music and dance floor, they must be subjected to a seemingly endless number of toasts, speeches, and dances. Unfortunately, most members of the wedding party are not practiced public speakers. Nor have they gotten the memo on how to script a crisp speech or toast. There are several activities expected to be standout moments: the bride and groom's first dance, the groom's speech and the FOTB speech and toast.

At some point during the festivities, make sure you've taken the MOTB for a slow spin on the dance floor. It is time to start thanking her for all her work to get the family to this good place. Flowers, wine, and spa days are great ways to say thank you. But a heartfelt, tender slow dance goes a long way with the MOTB.

The time you spend at the reception will go very quickly. An hour or so after food service is finished, you will notice people starting to leave.

As the FOTB and ambassador for the wedding, try to say good-bye and re-thank as many guests as you can. The gesture will be appreciated by the guests, and you will get kind words about the day from them as well.

I will always remember and cherish the parting comments from guests as they left my daughter's wedding. Those words made us feel that our obligation to host a great lifecycle event that would be memorable in our family history had been fulfilled, and all the effort and expense had been worthwhile.

During the last portion of the reception, as guests depart and the exit of the bride and groom is imminent, it is a natural time to take a deep breath and reflect. Survey the room, soak in the sight of your family having fun and being together as a united group. The years and lifetime memories will play in your head like an old movie for you to watch and savor. Cherish this moment, as it is something that makes being a FOTB and the life journey worth it.

Scene Six – BIG DEAL: FOTB Dance

One of the signature moments of the reception is the FOTB dance with the newly minted bride. This sounds like a straightforward item on the program and nothing much to worry about, right?

Like most of the reception program elements, the key is brevity and not making a fool of yourself.

The first question to answer is whether you are a good dancer. You don't need to be Bolshoi-trained but knowing which hand to lead with and the ability to muddle through a small, square box set of dance steps will suffice.

I am not a very good dancer and was terrified at the thought of performing in front of 150 friends and family. So, I did enlist a couple of remedies. The first was watching and practicing along with some slow-dance videos. In retrospect, I wish I had taken dance lessons, as many FOTBs do to best prepare for this moment.

The other tactic to lessen the risk of embarrassment was to minimize the amount of time on the dance floor. One of my appointed tasks as FOTB was to pick my dance song, and so, as mentioned previously, my first and driving consideration for the choice was length—shorter being better.

The next thing to consider was the song itself. Did it reflect the relationship between me and my daughter? Many choose some soppy, frilly tune talking about butterflies and unicorns. Other FOTBs prefer a song reflecting the love and goodness of life in this moment. Just like a good Valentine's Day card, the words should align with the rhythm of your life with your daughter. There are many playlists and potential songs available on the internet to aid your search.

After a couple of hours of online searching and general head- scratching, I came up with my perfect FOTB song. First of all, "What a Wonderful World" by Louis Armstrong is just a super-great song. The words are simple and elegant. The music is tranquil and comforting. When the song starts, wherever played, you can hear an audible "ahhhh" from the crowd and everyone smiles. It is the perfect celebratory slow dance tune, and it comes in at an economical 2 minutes and 17 seconds.

The last thing to remember is that the bride's dress most likely will impede any lively movement on your part. The dress may be draped on the floor and either one of you can step on it, creating a possible YouTube memory. Be careful, and get it done… Give the cameras their moment and move on to the next program item.

FOTB Survival Tactic #22 – Craft the FOTB dance to be a moment befitting the love between you and your daughter.

Scene Seven – BIG DEAL: Father of the Bride Speech

There are two vastly different but equally important occasions in a man's life when he may be called upon to speak. The first is at a child's wedding, and the second, at a parent's funeral. I am not trying to draw any analogies between the two, but rather to point out that these are likely the two most important speeches you'll ever make. You have to get them right.

Most people fear public speaking of any sort, so preparation is imperative to allay that fear. Your FOTB speech must be scripted and rehearsed to ensure a natural and comfortable feel on the wedding day. There are many on-line sites for an FOTB to consult on writing his speech. And as for other wedding services, there are also professionals available to aid you in writing your speech. It may be well worth the price to have this burden taken off your shoulders, especially if it is an area of fear and trepidation for you.

In constructing the speech, the first consideration is length. I am a firm believer in brevity. A good FOTB speech should not exceed much more than five minutes. Anything longer, and it will sound like a report or a sermon. Your speech is one only one of many the guests will be subjected to during the reception, so keep the festivities moving.

The three big areas to consider in getting your speech together are:

- Structure and Content
- Delivery Technique
- Practice

Let's tackle these one at a time... starting with **Structure and Content**. Like a well-written monologue or short story, the FOTB speech has three pieces: the introduction, the main body, and a conclusion.

In the **Introduction,** you want to set the tone for your conversation —yes, I like to think of it as a conversation— with the guests. First, remember, this is a friendly audience. This is not a hostile sales presentation or school board meeting. You know these people and hopefully have connected with most of them in some way by the time you get the microphone in your hand. Common elements of a good introduction might include:

- Thanking everyone for joining you; maybe call out a specific person or group of people.
- Acknowledging the great venue and hoping everyone is having a good time.
- Taking a moment to publicly thank your wife and daughter for putting the day together. Applause is a great ice breaker!
- Something witty or funny about the day you might have picked up in the last few hours.

During my FOTB speech, I went off-script immediately in the intro- duction. I started by saying how glad I was to have only one daughter and be responsible for only one wedding. There were some chuckles from the crowd as they thought I was referring to the cost of the affair.

I put my hand up as if to rebuff the negative notion about the wedding cost, and said, "I never realized how HARD it is to walk your daughter down that aisle."

I took a pause for about three long seconds, and then said, "The only thing that made it easier was knowing I was handing her over to the right man. And William... you are the right man."

After a little applause and lovely sighs from the guests, I moved into the main body of my speech.

The **Main Body** is NOT intended to be a complete encyclopedia and timeline of your daughter's life. Rather, you want to share why she is important to you and your wife. What are her endearing qualities? What are the different or challenging bits about her making her unique to the world? Using quick stories or anecdotes, share insights and special glimpses into your relationship with her. This is the platform for telling the world why you are proud of her... so do it.

To build your main body, I suggest a technique most writers use. Just sit with a piece of paper or a blank Word document and for ten minutes or so, let ideas flow. Don't regulate or edit. Just create a list of words that come to mind... or a couple of words that trigger a specific story about her. If you do this a couple of times, I guarantee you will have something you can start to assemble some thoughts about. Remember, you have only a handful of minutes, so impactful words or stories are the best.

The smaller piece of your main body is acknowledging your new son-in-law. Your knowledge and ability to speak about him depends on how long you've known him. Often, Mr. Right has been in the picture for a few years, so you've got some good fodder about him. The objective is to speak of him or share a story showing how he has become a member of your family and is a good match for your daughter.

In my situation, I shared with the crowd how my new son-in-law had enjoyed becoming a part of our family: he enjoyed staying at our lake house, he enjoyed our food, he enjoyed my cigars, he enjoyed my scotch, and he enjoyed it when I paid for dinner. Well, you get the picture. So, the punchline to this vignette was a pause on my part, and then I turned to look at him, and said, "William, I want you to memorize and say after me these three words...Let's go Dutch!" Of course, this lighthearted relationship dig at my new son got a pretty good reaction from the crowd. Always, note there is a fine line between humor and humiliation. Have fun and treat the groom as one of your own, but in a loving manner, not disrespectfully.

In addition to the son-in-law, this is a perfect time to acknowledge and speak about the new in-laws, and perhaps other people important to the newly married couple.

Your **Finish** to what has hopefully been a stirring FOTB speech is commonly a toast. There are many words and phrases to capture the sentiments, but the intent is to ask everyone to join in celebrating the marriage of the bride and groom and to welcome the in-law family into yours. Clink, clink!

After you've conquered structure and content, let's focus on **Delivery Technique**. A comfortable approach is to think of the FOTB speech as a conversation with your friends. Your delivery should be somewhat slow and measured. There is no need to speed up or machine-gun the words. Let each loving thought take time to settle in with the guests. Be sure to modulate your tone. Don't settle into a boring monotone.

This is an occasion when you want to be personal and intimate with your audience. If the reception venue has a lectern, I recommend trying not to use it. Either stand beside it or roam away from it. As part of the event preparation, I suggest having a mobile microphone requested for the speakers. Move around some and make connection with the guests... they won't bite.

As part of your preparation for delivering the speech, I suggest you physically write your speech out, either verbatim or with highlights or bullet points. I have spent a lot of time speaking during my career, and I chose not to wing it and wrote out a script. This five-minute conversation is way too important to ad-lib. All the great thoughts and stories you have stored in your mind don't easily come easily to your tongue in front of the guests at the reception.

You should write several drafts and read each one out loud. This exercise will help you **turn writing into spoken words**. When you are comfortable enough to do so, practice a time or two reading it to your wife or someone you trust. This doesn't have to be perfect; you are refining the messages, words, and timing. The more you rehearse the talk, the more relaxed and natural you will be.

Getting into the technical weeds for a moment.... When you decide to print out your final version, here are a couple of ideas. First, use a very large font. It should be large enough for you to read without reading glasses, if that is a possibility for you. Assume you might not have them, or just want to communicate without them.

Second, space the paragraphs or sentences so that a single sentence doesn't span a printed page. You are a speechwriter now and need to imagine how to make it easier to read. Minimize any possible risks, distractions, or hazards that will mess you up in front of an audience.

Many men see the FOTB speech as a torturous obligation and fear it. If you reframe it as an opportunity to celebrate your daughter and your family with others, you may regard it in a more positive light. Break the task down, invest the time, practice, and you will deliver a great speech and be the envy of others.

FOTB Survival Tactic #23 – *Plan and invest the time to make the speech right and comfortable— to make it yours*

Scene Eight – Farewell to the New Couple and End of the Evening

And now, after months of preparation, considerable financial backing, and untold frayed emotions, it is time to close the door on your daughter's wedding.

The emotional, if not official, end of the evening is the send-off for the bride and groom. Tradition dictates the couple run through a gauntlet of guests as they enter their getaway conveyance. At that point, most of the guests will depart and, depending on your arrangements with the reception venue, a part of the crowd might continue to party and enjoy company with new and old friends.

Hopefully during the day, you or your wife haven't misplaced the collection of tip envelopes. Your wedding planner will be the best source of who gets how much tip. There are quite a few service people who rely heavily on tips and hopefully have been delivering great service to deserve a tip. You and MOTB can divide and conquer with delivery of the tip money and a sincere message of thanks.

The next and somewhat tedious part of ending the reception is taking care of all the "stuff", which normally refers to the floral arrangements, leftover food, and the cake(s). Most of this is handled during the planning process.

Many venues have arrangements with local charities to take flowers for placement in nursing homes and similar settings. Likewise, I have seen leftover food donated to homeless shelters or kitchens. I found it amazing how creative people are and how willing to help others. It is truly a shame to let the flowers and food go to waste. If your flowers can brighten a nursing home setting for a few days, that's a good way to pay it forward.

Your daughter may or may not have changed out of her wedding dress prior to her escape with your newly minted son-in-law. So, you may have another passenger —the dress—in the car that night. I strongly advise FOTB and MOTB, if able, to each have a vehicle available at the reception for transporting all the residual items a wedding leaves behind.

Despite living in the time of digital wedding registries and Amazon, some guests will bring cards and presents to the wedding. Nice, but more space in the car will be taken up. If the bride and groom do not live in the same city as the wedding, arrangements will need to be made to transport the cards and presents to them.

Before closing the reception, there is one large, but hopefully unnecessary task remaining. As the FOTB, you are ambassador to and guardian over the flock of guests. So, you need to survey the remaining guests and see if any need assistance getting home or to a hotel. An abundance of caution is a good thing here. Have some cash, or a rideshare app ready to roll just in case. Everyone will feel better in the morning if you do.

The tabletop flower settings are usually desirable pieces the MOTB can give to guests willing to take them home that evening. Again, the objective is to keep your trunk as empty as possible going home.

Of course, there will be items you gain unplanned custody of, such as event signage.

The MOTB often takes custody of the remaining wedding cake and the all-important top layer. You will have the cake as a guest in your freezer until the newlyweds return from their honeymoon unless you're able to get it to their freezer immediately.

Whether you and the MOTB go home after closing the reception, to a friend's "after-party", or connect with others at the out-of-town guest HQ hotel, you deserve to enjoy the moment. Have that glass of good alcohol, and perhaps an occasion-worthy nod to a fine cigar—for attitude adjustment purposes only. Savor and enjoy this moment. Your friends and family should be sharing kind compliments and stories about the evening. After some time for reflection and appreciation, you can take your FOTB hat off and revert to just being a father and husband.

Congratulations... you survived.

BUT WAIT... what about the BIG payoff? Hopefully you weren't kept by other guests or some task from saying goodbye to the bride as she left. This is the moment you've worked for all these months, and the essence of what all the pages in this book have been written to build to. I know your love for your daughter is unconditional, but to get a hug and a kiss punctuated with the words, "I love you! Thank you for today!" is the greatest thanks a father can ever get.

Epilogue

The Day After

Vacuum... the absence of sound, energy, and emotion. This is the best way to describe the day after a wedding. Everyone is physically and emotionally spent, especially MOTB and FOTB. You probably have a few hours of obligations in the morning to perform tasks such as airport runs, breakfast, and maybe lunch with relatives.

But when you finally get home, it is time to collapse. I remember my wife and I went out and grabbed an early dinner and basically crashed for twelve hours straight. I strongly suggest planning an easy day of work the Monday after a weekend wedding to get your act together.

Also, you can help the MOTB with any remaining small errands or tasks to put the wedding to bed. One task of note is the tuxedo return. You might be burdened with collecting and returning the formal wear of some groomsmen who have jumped on planes back home. I always hated this bit, as accounting for all the pieces is fraught with error, and the garb is dirty and sweaty from the high-octane young men. Just ensure your credit card is not associated with these guys.

Next Step – Chart Your Personal Success as an FOTB

Hopefully, you have gained a greater appreciation for all the participants, players, and work needed to provide a great wedding for your daughter.

The stories and survival tactics in this book are intended to arm you and point out potential difficulties in the journey. Your special talents as a FOTB can add value to process and reduce your anxiety and fears. The wedding is a project that can have a timeline, task list, budget, and deliverables. Approaching the wedding as this type of project can produce a calmer frame of mind for you and a smoother relationship with the MOTB and bride.

For further insights, ideas, and camaraderie, please join the FOTB community at FatheroftheBride.org. When you visit the site, you will gain access to podcasts, articles, and website links for many of the specific topics and scenes found in this book.

I wish you success and look forward to you sharing your story as a future contributor to our FOTB community.

Appendix 1 – Draft Budget

Here is a draft budget template for you to build estimates and track the costs of your wedding. More detailed and downloadable templates are available at FatheroftheBride.org.

Wedding Budget

Wedding Date: July 16, 2024			Days Remaining: 365	
CATEGORY	**ESTIMATED**	**ACTUAL**		**OVER/UNDER**
Apparel	9,490.00	9,770.00	⬇	-280.00
Reception	1,050.00	928.00	⬆	122.00
Music	600.00	400.00	⬆	200.00
Printing	935.00	870.00	⇔	65.00
Photography	1,625.00	1,575.00	⇔	50.00
Decorations	700.00	720.00	⇔	-20.00
Flowers	900.00	850.00	⇔	50.00
Gifts	1,345.00	1,075.00	⬆	270.00
Travel	100.00	165.00	⇔	-65.00
Other	885.00	1,021.00	⬇	-136.00
Total expenses	**17,630.00**	**17,374.00**		**256.00**

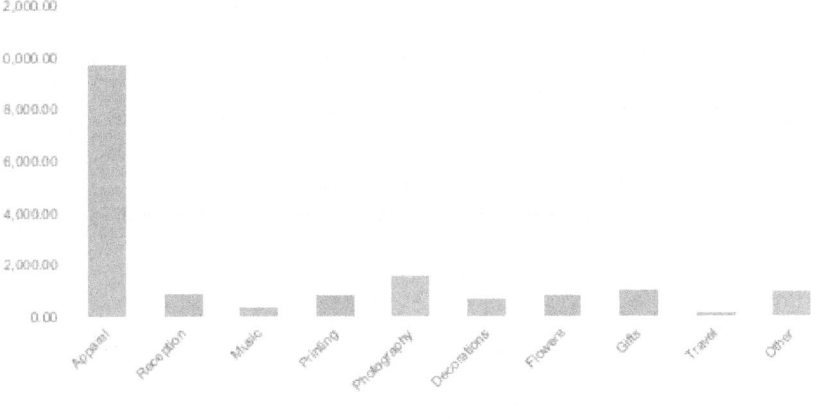

Appendix 2 – Questions for the Caterer at Wedding Food Tasting

If the engaged couple has a food tasting at the proposed reception venue prior to finalizing the contract, it's best to make the most of the opportunity. There are several key questions to ask that will put the families at ease.

- *Who is preparing the tasting today?*

Possibly the most important thing to ask at a tasting. A company might have one skilled chef who does all of the tastings but won't be cooking at your event.

- *How far is the kitchen from where my guests will be dining?*

Some food doesn't hold up as well as others, so you may need to design a menu that works at room temperature. Weather should be taken into consideration. Food gets cold much more quickly in a cold or possibly winter setting.

- *How do you handle dietary restrictions and allergies*

Caterers can usually handle most dietary restrictions or allergies with enough notice. You just need to understand what the requirements are for building the questions into the invitation process.

While these are the key questions to be asked, there are some additional items to be questioned:

- Can we meet the on-site coordinator before the wedding day?
- Can we see photos of the food and presentation from some of your past events?
- How many weddings do you typically do in a year?
- Do you supply linens and napkins? What are the costs?
- What is the server to guest ratio?
- Does our venue have enough kitchen space for you to deliver our menu?
- Where do you source your food from?
- How will everything be plated, portioned, and presented on the day of the event?
- When do you need final menu choices and headcount?
- Do you provide bartending services? If so, do you provide the alcohol?
- Are non-alcoholic beverages included in the food costs? If not, what are those costs?
- What is your cancellation policy?

About the Author

Michael Slavin wishes he had been more informed and prepared for his Father-of-the-Bride (FOTB) journey. As an FOTB alumnus, Michael chose the FOTB topic for a book as it is one of the most important events in a father's life. In addition to his life as a father, grandfather, and IT consultant, Michael enjoys sharing his and others' experiences in writing and via a on-line community. Michael can be contacted at mike@fatherofthebride.org.

You can connect with me on:
 ✪ http://www.fatherofthebride.org

Printed in Great Britain
by Amazon